THOMAS KINKADE

with
Anne Christian Buchanan

Just Around the Bend

HARVEST HOUSE PUBLISHERS

EUGENE, OREGON

Just Around the Bend

Text Copyright © 2002 by Media Arts Group, Inc., Morgan Hill, CA 95037
and Harvest House Publishers, Eugene OR 97402

Published by Harvest House Publishers
Eugene, OR 97402

Just around the bend / [compiled by] Thomas Kinkade with
     Anne Christian Buchanan.
     p.cm.—(Simpler times collection)
     ISBN 0-7369-0926-5
       1. Religion—Quotations, maxims, etc. 2. Conduct of life—Quotations,
     maxims, etc. I. Kinkade, Thomas, 1958- II. Buchanan, Anne Christian.

PN6084.R3 J87 2002
082—dc21

                                                            2001059418

Text from this book has been excerpted from *Simpler Times* by
Thomas Kinkade (Harvest House Publishers, 1996)

Verses are taken from the Holy Bible, New International Version®. Copyright
© 1973, 1978, 1994 by the International Bible Society. Used by permission
of Zondervan Publishing House.

Design and production by Koechel Peterson & Associates, Minneapolis,
Minnesota

Printed in Hong Kong

02 03 04 05 06 07 08 09 10 11/ NG / 10 9 8 7 6 5 4 3 2 1

You have made known to me the path of life;

you will fill me with joy in your presence,

with eternal pleasures at your right hand.

—THE BOOK OF PSALMS

As a child, I was endlessly exploring the brown grassy hillsides and oak-dotted meadows around my hometown of Placerville. My best times came when my brother Pat and I set out on our bikes with sketchbooks and sandwiches and a dayful of endless hours in our pockets to spend as we pleased. We memorized sights and sounds. We collected experiences. We lived in the moment, with tomorrow always tantalizingly around the bend.

In those days of boyhood freedom, my heart dreamed of moving past my own familiar haunts. I longed to go further, to see more, to explore places I had never dreamed of.

Even then, I had a hobo's heart.

Afoot and light-hearted I take to the open road,

Healthy, free, the world before me,

The long brown path before me leading

wherever I choose.

—WALT WHITMAN

For me, it's the twists and the turns and the curves and surprises that make the journey of life more meaningful and more fun. Some of life's most important lessons, its most resplendent joys, happen when you put yourself in the path of serendipity.

For me, a hobo's heart is an attitude, a set of mind. It's an insatiable curiosity, a chronic itch to discover what's out there beyond your own backyard, a breathless anticipation over what might be around the next bend of life's road.

I quickly learned that being an artist is a perfect excuse for being a hobo. An artist is by definition a collector of experience. And there's always another vista around the bend, beckoning an artist to see the world from another perspective. So it was that as I grew, my artistic ambitions kept my heart on the road—although I suspect I would have been an explorer anyway.

Do not go where the path may lead; go instead where there is no path and leave a trail.

— RALPH WALDO EMERSON

Faith is like radar that sees through the fog—the reality of things at a distance that the human eye cannot see.

—CORRIE TEN BOOM

Thomas
Kinkade

It was while I was a student that I started the practice of going on "hoists" with my friend James Gurney. "Hoist" was our makeshift word for a sketching adventure—an excursion with sketchpads to a mountaintop, a train yard, a small town, an inner-city neighborhood. We relished the surprise and adventure of it. We never knew where we would end up. And we filled both our sketchbooks and our memories with unforgettable people and places.

Then came the ultimate hoist, when we actually did become hobo artists, riding the rails cross-country and sketching as we went. Eventually we wrote a book about what we saw and learned, but writing a book wasn't what we set out to do. What we set out to do was explore, to see what we could see. What we set out to do was to follow our hobo's hearts.

If one advances confidently in the direction of his dreams, and endeavors to live the life which he has imagined, he will meet with a success unexpected in common hours.

— HENRY DAVID THOREAU

I've been doing it ever since, even as I worked to develop my career, to establish a company, to raise a family. That's why one Christmas found our entire family in a rented RV, tooling our way around the deserts of California. We set aside an entire week with no agenda except painting and exploration. When we wanted to stop, we found a campground and let the children play in the pool. When we saw an intriguing side road, we followed it. When the sunset painted the desert soft and red and cast intriguing shadows under the rocks and the Joshua trees, we stopped and painted—or just sat and watched.

When the week was over, we came back home to our "normal" life. Merritt returned to school. Chandler and baby Winsor played and learned. Nanette cooked and mounted canvases and cared for the family, and I painted and signed prints and did business.

But we were already dreaming of the next time we'd be on the road. And already we were wondering what the next turn in life would bring.

Adventure is worthwhile in itself.

—AMELIA EARHART

Thomas
Kinkade

I am supremely blessed to be married to a woman who shares my wandering spirit. Ever since we were married, we have had the privilege of being hoboes together. Before the girls were born, we traveled the world with backpacks and sketchbooks. When our family began to grow, our luggage list did, too, but we didn't stop going on adventures. We simply packed up the girls and took them with us. I have hiked innumerable trails with a baby in a backpack and a chubby little hand holding on to mine.

It has certainly made our life incredibly richer. And it couldn't have happened if we hadn't made the commitment to cultivating a hobo's heart.

One of the reasons we try to keep such a close watch on our time commitments is that we are committed to making space for serendipity. We don't want our life packed so full that we are too busy to explore or too jaded to want a surprise.

Direct me in the path of your commands, for there I find delight. Turn my heart toward your statutes and not toward selfish gain.

—THE BOOK OF PSALMS

Thomas Kinkade

We must get beyond textbooks, go out into the bypaths and untrodden depths of the wilderness and travel and explore and tell the world the glories of our journey.

—JOHN HOPE FRANKLIN

How can you go exploring when every minute is planned?

How can you have surprises when every hour is scheduled?

We leave sizable gaps in our schedule for road trips and family outings. We ration the time and energy we spend on outside commitments and after-school activities in order to lavish our time and energy on planning our next excursion.

We plan in order to experience the joy of anticipation, but a lot of our planning involves a lot of not planning. We decide where we'll go to start—to the mountains or to the desert or to Italy or to the little park five miles away. And we may decide where our home base will be—perhaps a rented RV or a campsite or a cabin or home. From there, though, we stop planning. Or rather, our plan is not to plan.

Whenever we hit the hobo road, we defer to the spirit of serendipity.

We reserve the right to travel byroads on a whim, to cancel one set of plans in favor of a completely different one, to spend an entire day in one spot instead of pushing on to where we thought we'd go. We take risks on possibilities rather than sure things.

Often, the unexpected happens. I can still see us standing by a cold Montana roadside next to a dead steer and a totaled pickup truck loaded with camping gear—Nanette four months pregnant, me wondering how we would make it back to town.

And I can see the two of us standing on a crooked little cobblestone street in Italy, staring ruefully at a broken rain gutter while a tiny old woman gave us a thorough tongue-lashing in Italian we couldn't understand. Our borrowed RV, trying to maneuver in the narrow space between overhanging roofs, had scraped the gutter and left it dangling. We had visions of spending the night in a little Italian jail.

I expect to pass through this world but once; any good thing, therefore, that I can do, or any kindness that I can show to my fellow creatures, let me do it now; let me not defer or neglect it, for I shall not pass this way again.

—STEPHEN GRELLET

Then they said to him, "Please inquire of God to learn whether our journey will be successful." The priest answered them, "Go in peace. Your journey has the LORD's approval."

THE BOOK OF JUDGES

And yet the alchemy of memory has managed to turn even these moments into golden experience. The wreck in Montana left us unhurt and eventually led to a wonderful experience of painting in West Yellowstone with an old friend and a new friend who let us stay in his home. The incident of the broken rain gutter ended up costing about seven dollars—and it still makes us laugh. The way we look at it, we have very little to lose by putting ourselves in the path of serendipity.

If we hadn't been willing to rent an Irish cottage sight unseen, for example, we would have missed the lovely sapphire lake set in brilliant green, the simple but cozy accommodations, the ruined castles around the bend. We would never have attended the village singalong and sat rapt while children danced and grandparents told stories and the whole town joined in the singing.

Heaven is under our feet as well as

over our heads.

— HENRY DAVID THOREAU

Real joy comes not from ease or riches or from the praise

of men, but from doing something worthwhile.

—SIR WILFRED GRENFELL

Thomas Kinkade

If we hadn't been willing to ask questions and jump at opportunities, we would never have been able to spend two weeks painting in Norman Rockwell's old studio, looking at the world as that great painter saw it, trying to see the landscape through his eyes. Or we would have missed the lovely Chinese festival of lanterns—the whole village lit with tiny paper lanterns—which we happened upon by accident in Monterey, California.

For us, the rich dimensions such experiences give to our lives are worth any inconvenience we may encounter from not knowing ahead of time what's going to happen. They are worth the sacrifices we must make to keep our time free for travel and discovery.

And that's true for you as well, whether or not your budget or schedule allows for distant adventures. The same eye for exploration that carries you far from home can also carry you joyfully through your days closer to home.

You can take a family jaunt to the little town thirty miles away. Hang out in the local coffee shop. Poke around in that little antique shop you've driven by a dozen times on your way to someplace you've planned to go. Pack along your camera and your notebook and your sketchbook. For the cost of a tank of gas and a paper sack of sandwiches you can have an adventure to remember.

If you have a hobo's heart and a spirit of adventure, you can turn a walk through the neighborhood into an excursion. If you know a child, ask him or her for assistance. Children so often know the secret of finding wonder in the most common places.

Wisdom is to finish the moment, to find the journey's end in every step of the road, to live the greatest number of good hours.

—RALPH WALDO EMERSON

You don't even need to go out of doors in order to go exploring. If you are willing to let your spirit wander free, an afternoon at the art museum can be an unforgettable adventure. An evening with a good book can be a trek into the unknown. An hour spent with an intriguing companion can be an adventurous journey—for what is more mysterious and full of surprise than the human soul?

Like most other aspects of simpler times, exploration and discovery and serendipity depend more on your frame of mind than on your circumstances. You will make discoveries, you will enjoy adventures, because you are willing to open your eyes and your heart to discovery and adventure.

Adventure is not outside a man; it is within.

—DAVID GRAYSON

A work of art is above all an adventure of the mind.

—EUGENE IONESCO

And then, in the process, something else will happen—or at least that has been my experience.

As you set out into your world with a hobo's heart, your world will grow larger. And you will be growing, too. As you encounter challenges along your way, you will grow stronger. As you adjust your route in response to your circumstances, you will grow more flexible. As you learn to treat adversity as an adventure, you will grow more hopeful, less afraid, better equipped to cope with what life throws your way.

The habit of following the twisting road, of walking with a spirit of excited anticipation, of rolling with the punches and stepping around the rocks—all these are important skills for carrying you safely through your life.

My favorite thing is to go

where I've never been.

—DIANE ARBUS

And this, of course, is the secret—the reason life is simpler when you follow a hobo's heart.

The surprises will come, regardless. The unexpected will happen. And if you're living in anticipation, making room for the unexpected, you know the joy of the road. You will be a traveler, not a refugee. You will be moving forward, not just moving along.

And I guarantee there will be wonderful surprises waiting for you—just around the bend.

Be not afraid of life. Believe that life is worth living, and your belief will help create the fact.

—WILLIAM JAMES

Life's a voyage that's homeward bound.

—HERMAN MELVILLE

Your word is a lamp to my

feet and a light for my path.

—THE BOOK OF PSALMS

Thomas
Kinkade